ABUNDANT TRUTH INTERNATIONAL MINISTRIES

Abundant Truth International's Inspirational Series

PERSEVERANCE UNDER PRESSURE

Maintaining Faith While You Wait

Mister Roderick L. Evans

Perseverance under Pressure
Maintaining Faith and Endurance in Challenging Times

All Rights Reserved © 2024 by Roderick L. Evans

No part of this book may be reproduced or transmitted in any form or by any means, graphic, electronic, or mechanical, including photocopying, recording, taping, or by any information storage or retrieval system, without the permission in writing from the publisher.

Front & Back Cover Designs by Abundant Truth Publishing
Image by Alex Peroff from Pixabay

Abundant Truth Publishing
an imprint of Abundant Truth International Ministries

For information address:
Abundant Truth International
P.O. Box 126
Camden, NC 27921

ISBN: 978-1-60141-640-7

Printed in the United States of America

Unless otherwise indicated all of the scripture quotations are taken from the Authorized King James Version of the Bible. Scripture quotations marked with NIV are taken from the New International Version of the Bible. Scriptures marked with NASV are taken for the New American Standard Version of the Bible.

Contents

Introduction

Chapter 1 – The Function of Pressure   1
Reveals Weakness/Strengths   6
Believers and Benevolence   8

Chapter 2 – Prayer and Praise   17
Prayer   20
Perpetual Praise   22

Chapter 3 – Peers   33
Called to Community   37
Do Not Disconnect   39
God Has a Remnant   41

Contents (cont.)

Chapter 4 – Divine Purpose	53
Be Steadfast	55
Be Faithful	57
Bibliography	67

Introduction

The Christian life is simple and complex simultaneously. Its simplicity rests upon one truth: Jesus Christ is the Son of God and that faith in Him results in man's salvation. However, to live a fruitful Christian life comes from navigating through the complexities of life.

The Abundant Truth Inspirational Series was developed to aid the Christian in handling the difficulties that come with the Christian experience.

In this publication:

The bible contains numerous passages describing the trials, tests, and tribulations that accompany the Christian life and experience. However, believers are encouraged to stand in faith and hope even during difficult circumstances and situations.

In this *book, we want to offer encouragement and hope to Christians who are experiencing difficult circumstances. Embrace faith and endurance in your challenging situations.

- This book is the transcription of a teaching done during the pandemic. The videos of this teaching can be found at http://bit.ly/3Efz7FH.

PERSEVERRANCE UNDER PRESSURE

Maintaining Faith and Endurance in Challenging Times

-Chapter 1-

The Function of Pressure

PERSEVERRANCE UNDER PRESSURE
Maintaining Faith and Endurance in Challenging Times

Maintaining Faith and Endurance in Challenging Times

We want to begin our discussion by referring to II Timothy 2:3,

Thou therefore endure hardness, as a good soldier of Jesus Christ.

Our focus for this publication will be Perseverance under Pressure. We know that in this day and time we have now moved into a time of a pandemic.

The pandemic obviously has caused extra pressure on our finances, on how we deal with one another socially and even upon how we worship.

But we must know and understand

that our faith in Jesus Christ has given us the ability that we can persevere under pressure.

When we look in the scriptures, we find that every time Jesus spoke to his disciples, he would always warn them of troublesome times, of how they would be hated, how the world would come against them.

But he also told them that he was going to be with them, that you can tell that even in Him speaking to them, he did not tell them that the troubles would not come. He told them to expect the trouble, but also to maintain their faith.

Because it is so easy that as pressure is being applied, for people to forget the faith and its foundation. And so, it is my intent to challenge people to know that they can still maintain good perseverance even under pressure.

And so, I just want to leave just three main points with you in this publication to encourage you to know that, hey, I can persevere under pressure.

And that with these three things, if you keep them in mind, it should help you keep a focus. I want to lay the foundation of the purpose of pressure. When pressure comes, it has a twofold benefit.

Reveals Weakness/Strengths

One thing, it reveals your weaknesses to yourself. But the opposite of that, it shows you how strong you really are.

Sometimes you never really know what you can go through until you go through it. Because oftentimes we'll say, I just don't think I can handle it, well you really don't know that. That is only fear talking.

Because I can't know I can't handle it,

unless I go through it and don't handle it. But many Christians can testify, many things that we thought we could not handle, we've handled it.

It is because the Lord brought us through. It is funny that Israel, when you look at their plight in the wilderness, as much as they complain, even though they move from hardship to hardship, God still told them, I bore you up on eagle's wings. That even though they had to go through those things, God brought them through all right.

And so, the Christian can believe and

know that even though we are in some hard times and, the thing about it is, the church has added pressure.

Because not only do we have the pressure of the sinful world against our faith, but now it wants to pressure us and try to criticize our good works.

Believers and Benevolence

I saw a post one time where the article writer tried to say that people that were non-Christians were more "Christian" than Christians. How absurd is that statement?

PERSEVERRANCE UNDER PRESSURE

Maintaining Faith and Endurance in Challenging Times

Because the thing that first of all defines a Christian is salvation in Jesus Christ. The first thing that defines a Christian is to be renewed by the blood of Jesus Christ.

The thing that defines a person as a Christian is a transformed life. And then it's only out of that transformed life that we do good works. But we don't do good works to verify we are Christians. We do good works just **because** we are Christians.

Let your light so shine before men, that they may see your good works, and glorify your Father which is in heaven. (Matthew 5:16)

Christians sometimes, in our attempt to show forth a good example, will forget about the very foundation and core of our Christianity.

It's not in what we do, it's first of all in who we are. And if we become who we ought to be in Christ, we're going to do what we need to do.

Because you can see that sometimes churches can begin to try to do stuff to compete with the world. We're not in competition with the world. We've already won. Because we believe because we've already gained eternal life.

And so, I just wanted to share that because during these times, people can say, "Well, the church got so much money. Why isn't it doing more?" We can't save the world. The sinners have a whole lot of money. They're not giving up all their money either.

The logic is flawed. Because if I'm supposed to be a good Christian and do it, then a good sinner is supposed to do the same thing because sinners are bankrolling their lifestyle.

And so, I feel for pastors that get under pressure to try to exhaust what they need to do for the local church for trying to compete with the world.

I've said it before, and I'll say it again. The churches are not designed to be social services. We are not designed that way. We are an entity of believers that are set aside to do that which is right to offer salvation.

And then if we can, out of our abundance and out of our resources, we will help anybody that needs it. But that is not our chief mandate.

The chief mandate of the church is to preach the gospel of Jesus Christ and offer salvation.

PERSEVERRANCE UNDER PRESSURE
Maintaining Faith and Endurance in Challenging Times

Maintaining Faith and Endurance in Challenging Times

Notes:

PERSEVERRANCE UNDER PRESSURE

Maintaining Faith and Endurance in Challenging Times

_____

_____

_____

_____

_____

_____

_____

_____

_____

_____

PERSEVERRANCE UNDER PRESSURE

Maintaining Faith and Endurance in Challenging Times

-Chapter 2-

Prayer and Praise

PERSEVERRANCE UNDER PRESSURE
Maintaining Faith and Endurance in Challenging Times

PERSEVERRANCE UNDER PRESSURE
Maintaining Faith and Endurance in Challenging Times

So now our text, we find here that Paul is writing to Timothy. And I only used the one verse because the one verse sums up our focus. We know Timothy. Paul was sending Timothy to different churches to help them in the faith.

But when Timothy was in these assemblies, he would find that people would show up with all kinds of doctrines.

Obviously, some people were challenging him because of his age. But Paul told him not to pray that it stopped, but to endure it.

And so even though as believers, we

know that things are going to happen, and God will allow some things to come upon us. But because they come upon us, that doesn't give us a reason to quit or to pull back from the faith.

And so, for our present discussion, I wanted just to give three points of how you are to persevere under pressure.

Prayer

The first thing you need in order to persevere under pressure is prayer. 1 Thessalonians 5, it tells us to pray without ceasing. And then it goes on to say, in everything give thanks, for this is the will of

God concerning you in Christ Jesus. That's in verses 17 and 18 of chapter 5.

So, we find here that Paul encourages the believers, and he said, what you have to do, you cannot stop praying because it's so easy when pressure sets in to throw off prayer for what I know.

In addition, to throw off prayer for my ingenuity. And anytime you throw off prayer, ungodly things become an option.

When I stop trusting God for the finances, I may resort to trickery and gambling. I may resort to lying on taxes to get extra money because I've stopped praying and trusting in God.

Prayer is what I like to call a "godly distraction." Prayer puts your attention on God and his power. I pray to God because He has the power to do any and everything.

Perpetual Praise

The second thing is in those verses that I quoted it says in everything give thanks. When you give thanks, it gets you off complaining and to begin to focus on then the presence of God.

The scriptures they show us that any

any time the praises of God are there, His power is there to accomplish and do great things.

> *And at midnight Paul and Silas prayed, and sang praises unto God: and the prisoners heard them. And suddenly there was a great earthquake, so that the foundations of the prison were shaken: and immediately all the doors were opened, and every one's bands were loosed. (Acts 16:25-26)*

Yet, sometimes we start falling off in prayer because we will say well I prayed before and it didn't happen, I prayed this many years and it didn't happen, but Jesus foreseeing how we are and how we would run into that predicament, He gave us the parable of the woman with the unjust judge.

> *And he spake a parable unto them to this end, that men ought always to pray, and not to faint; Saying, There was in a city a judge, which feared not God, neither regarded man: And there was a widow in that city; and she came unto him, saying, Avenge me of mine adversary. And he would not for a while: but afterward he said within*

himself, Though I fear not God, nor regard man; Yet because this widow troubleth me, I will avenge her, lest by her continual coming she weary me. (Luke 18:1-5)

The woman kept going and going and going and going and He said, at some point in time, the man though he was wicked heard her because she was persistent.

He then gave another parable of how when a man got some unexpected guest at his house, and he goes to his friend and says listen I'm going to need for you to help me I got some guests.

And he said unto them, Which of you shall have a friend, and shall go unto him at midnight, and say unto him, Friend, lend me three loaves; For a friend of mine in his journey is come to me, and I have nothing to set before him? And he from within shall answer and say, Trouble me not: the door is now shut, and my children are with me in bed; I cannot rise and give thee. I say unto you, Though he will not rise and give him, because he is his friend, yet because of his importunity he will rise and give him as many as he needeth. (Luke 11:5-8)

In their culture, you know hospitality was a big thing. So, if you receive somebody, you will want to treat them well. He said it is late; they were unexpected and I'm going to need some provisions for them.

The man, first of all, responded and said look I'm in bed and my family is in bed. I am not going to do this. The friend would not leave the door, Jesus then said the man did not get up because they were friends but because he was persistent.

PERSEVERRANCE UNDER PRESSURE
Maintaining Faith and Endurance in Challenging Times

We must remember that God is for us and not against us, but know and understand that if we keep coming God is going to do it because he really loves us and that he really is for us. You cannot allow pressure to cause you to stop praying and resort to other things:

1. to resort to the comfort of worry
2. to resort to the comfort of complaining
3. to resort to duplicity in your dealings in order to try to make up the slack.

When there are needs involved, you must know and understand that you can persevere under those pressure if you maintain your prayer life. Prayer not only gives us access to God, but prayer also strengthens us.

I said at the beginning of this publication that prayer is a godly distraction because it takes your mind off your circumstances. Remember, as you pray, you are supposed to be releasing your burdens to the Lord.

Moreover, as you praise Him, you are saying, "I praise you because I understand that in Your greatness. You are going to be greater than whatever pressures are upon me presently."

Notes:

PERSEVERRANCE UNDER PRESSURE
Maintaining Faith and Endurance in Challenging Times

PERSEVERRANCE UNDER PRESSURE

Maintaining Faith and Endurance in Challenging Times

-Chapter 3-

Peers

PERSEVERRANCE UNDER PRESSURE

Maintaining Faith and Endurance in Challenging Times

The third thing that is going to help you to persevere under pressure is your peers when I say peers I mean the community of believers. When we get saved God is so good that he just does not save us alone.

When I am saved, I am alone and it's a soul thing between me and God. However, God does not leave us alone. God will place us among other believers.

But now hath God set the members every one of them in the body, as it hath pleased him. (1 Corinthians 12:18)

He will place us in the household of faith he gives us pastors and elders and ministers and those that will lead us and we have to be mindful that just because things aren't going our way, we can leave our fellowship with other Christians. Remember, it is among the believers that God will speak.

It is among the company of disciples that God will show himself mighty and strong. Hebrews 10:25 says not forsaking the assembling of yourselves as the manner of some is it says but rather exhort one another in so much the more as you see the day approaching.

Called to Community

The writer of Hebrews is telling us is that you need the assembly. I know people who love to say I do not need the church. Well, you are kind of going against God's whole plan and purpose.

God saves us and baptizes us into the Body by His Spirit, that we can only function and thrive in God as we stay connected to the Body.

I have met people through the years that say I do not need the church. That is an ungodly attitude.

If the spirit baptizes me into the body how is the spirit going to tell me not to be among the body? When you separate from the Body you may end up facing unnecessary pressure.

It is because we will not allow the household of faith to help us through pressure. Even during this time where everybody is going through the same thing, trust me, there is still strength in the house of God.

PERSEVERRANCE UNDER PRESSURE

Maintaining Faith and Endurance in Challenging Times

We know during this time with social distancing, some assemblies are not meeting, and some assemblies have resorted to doing ministry virtually.

Do Not Disconnect

Well, you still need to stay connected to your local church, even if it is by way of Zoom or any other media connection. Make sure that you are not throwing off coming together.

Also remember, when I say forsake not the assembling of yourselves, that means also do not also forsake your leaders, don't forsake your pastors.

PERSEVERRANCE UNDER PRESSURE
Maintaining Faith and Endurance in Challenging Times

If God has given you a pastor and a leader, then they are there to help you trust me God is Grace pastors and leaders that even though they are going through, there is a **grace** upon them that they can help you even in the midst of your pressure, but don't use perilous times to stay home.

Avoid these common reasons for staying home.

1. When we get "sick," we stay home.

2. When we do not think we have the right amount of money, we stay home

3. If the church is trying to do fundraising and we may not have that amount we stay home

We use a lot of trivial things to cause us to forsake coming together; and, especially during hard times we have to know the only way what's there to help you is the assembly of other Christians.

Trust me, the scriptures have always said that God never leaves Himself without a witness in the earth when you look at Biblical history.

God Has A Remnant

God has always had some people

among on this planet that served them I think one biblical account proves this point.

I remember the story of Abram that as he was traveling with Sarah, who was beautiful, and he was always afraid.

Say, I pray thee, thou art my sister: that it may be well with me for thy sake; and my soul shall live because of thee. (Genesis 12:13)

He feared that somebody would want to kill him and take her, but we find that when he went among a certain people, the king, Abimelech had taken his wife.

God came to the king and said I am going to kill you if you don't give that man back his wife because he's a prophet. The king said I did not know that that's who he was, but He said give Sarah back.

And Abraham journeyed from thence toward the south country, and dwelled between Kadesh and Shur, and sojourned in Gerar. And Abraham said of Sarah his wife, She is my sister: and Abimelech king of Gerar sent, and took Sarah. But God came to Abimelech in a dream by night, and said to him, Behold, thou art but a dead man, for the woman which thou hast taken; for she is a man's wife. But Abimelech had not come near her: and he said, Lord, wilt thou slay also a righteous nation? Said he not unto me, She is my sister? and she, even she herself said, He is my brother: in the integrity of my heart and innocency of my hands have I done this. *And God said unto him in a dream, Yea, I know that thou didst this in the integrity of thy heart; for I also withheld thee from sinning against me: therefore suffered I thee not to touch her. Now therefore restore the man his wife; for he is a prophet, and he shall pray for thee, and thou shalt live: and if thou restore her not, know thou that thou shalt surely die, thou, and all that are thine. Therefore Abimelech rose early in the morning, and called all his servants, and told all these things in their ears: and the men were sore afraid. Then Abimelech called Abraham, and said unto him, What hast thou done unto us? and what have I offended thee, that thou hast brought on me and on my kingdom a great sin? thou hast done deeds unto me that ought not to be done. And Abimelech said unto Abraham, What sawest thou, that thou hast done this thing? And Abraham said, Because I thought, Surely the fear of God is not in this place; and they will slay me for my wife's sake. (Genesis 20:1-11)*

When the king asked Abraham what did you see to cause you to lie why did you think you had to lie? Abraham said because I thought that the fear of the Lord was not in the place. Even during those times God still had people that served God.

They (Abraham and Abimelech) did not recognize that they were servants of God. This shows us that you must trust and know that there are Christians on this earth.

Hopefully, if you are a member of a local church and a local assembly, you can trust your brothers and sisters that are there.

Even if you have had problems, and you may have not liked what people have said and done, but if God be God, God has always left people in some of the strangest places.

PERSEVERRANCE UNDER PRESSURE
Maintaining Faith and Endurance in Challenging Times

Remember the verses in Book of Revelation when Jesus sent His angel to John and had him to write to the churches.

> *Thou hast a few names even in Sardis which have not defiled their garments; and they shall walk with me in white: for they are worthy. (Revelation 3:40*

One of the churches the churches was in bad shape, but He said that some in this assembly had endured, meaning that everybody in this assembly was not wrong. You can trust that if you are a member of a local church and if you believe that you are to be there, first of all trust your pastor.

Second of all trust that God will have some people in the assembly that are set aside that you can join hands with and that you all can encourage one another in the faith. Don't try to just persevere under pressure by yourself because you don't have to.

PERSEVERRANCE UNDER PRESSURE

Maintaining Faith and Endurance in Challenging Times

PERSEVERRANCE UNDER PRESSURE
Maintaining Faith and Endurance in Challenging Times

Notes:

_____

_____

_____

_____

_____

_____

_____

_____

_____

PERSEVERRANCE UNDER PRESSURE
Maintaining Faith and Endurance in Challenging Times

_____

_____

_____

_____

_____

_____

_____

_____

_____

_____

_____

-Chapter 4-

Divine Purpose

PERSEVERRANCE UNDER PRESSURE
Maintaining Faith and Endurance in Challenging Times

The final thing that we have to think about in persevering under pressure is you got to remember purpose. It is interesting to note that when trials, tests, and things come, we can think that God's original purpose has somehow been changed; or maybe, we have misheard or maybe I've been misled or maybe it's just not for me.

Be Steadfast

Paul wrote to the Corinthian church,

Therefore, my beloved brethren, be ye stedfast, unmoveable, always abounding in the work of the Lord, forasmuch as ye know that your labour is not in vain in the Lord. (I Corinthians 15 58)

You find that Paul says that you have to always be steadfast not only when things are going your way. When the pandemic began the Spirit spoke to me. He said these things may be a disruption of your lifestyle, but they are not a disruption of your purpose.

He said though you may have to do things differently on a daily basis, He said, but the purpose that God has still stands sure, even though we're going through all of these things.

Churches are in an uproar, jobs are in an uproar, but if God gave you a promise before the pandemic, somehow God is going to fulfill that 'promise even in the middle of the pandemic.

You got to know if God has called you, this is not the time to say, "Well I don't need to answer the call." NO! this is the perfect time for you to answer the call of God.

Be Faithful

Whatever God has told you to do in

your local church, for your local pastors, and for your local assemblies do that! Sometimes, we think that because I have so much stuff going on there is no way in the world, I can fulfill God's purpose.

If God has called you the missions at some point in time you are going to reach the mission field. Even if it is virtually. If God has said you have been called you to the Nations, you may not presently be able to step foot in those lands. But due to modern technology, you can reach a whole lot of places.

PERSEVERRANCE UNDER PRESSURE
Maintaining Faith and Endurance in Challenging Times

Even if your physical body is not there, God has a way of making sure that if He's spoken something to you, that word is going to endure regardless of whatever it is that you are facing in this life.

You find in the scriptures that the servants of God always face setbacks and obstacles as they try to fulfill the will of God.

Many are the afflictions of the righteous: but the Lord delivereth him out of them all. (Psalm 34:19)

Remember God anointed David through Samuel as king. He was in the palace and then he had to flee for his life, and he was a fugitive for a little while.

Because God had a purpose for him, God still brought him full circle. Even though we are in the midst of these trying times.

We are, in the midst of which seems like everything's stopped, but your purpose hasn't stopped. God will give you ideas. He will cause you to be creative to do what God has called you to do abroad and in the local church.

For those that may have ministries outside of their local church God will give you ways and means to accomplish it.

This is not the time to quit, this is not the time to think that the prophetic Spirit by whom God may have spoken to you personally, or spoken to you by others it was in error.

Obstacles never mean that the promises are obsolete. Physical pains do not mean that the purposes of God somehow have been aborted.

Do not think because you have got to slow down, that you have got to stop. Do not stop continue to pursue the plan and purpose of God for your life.

You have to know and understand that in this day and time the world wants us to quit. to so that we can say They want to say there was nothing to our faith all along.

However, that is untrue, it is a deception from the spirit of the Antichrist. We must know and understand that what we have believed is sure and it is on a firm foundation which is Jesus Christ

I just want to encourage you, in this publication, to know that you can persevere under pressure. Yes, pressure comes, and pressure sometimes is designed to try and stop you.

However, I think that sometimes a "good" pressure comes to show you that you can stand and that you can take it.

Many of us remember all of the beginning hardships of the pandemic, when they started giving us a lot of restrictions and things we had to do, and it seemed like we couldn't do it.

I can do all things through Christ which strengtheneth me. (I Corinthians 4:13)

PERSEVERRANCE UNDER PRESSURE
Maintaining Faith and Endurance in Challenging Times

Even after all of these years, we're still standing God is still on the throne. We are still here so that you can know and understand that you as the believer that you can persevere under pressure. Don't leave your local churches and don't leave the faith.

As we conclude this discussion, remember that you can Persevere under Pressure.

PERSEVERRANCE UNDER PRESSURE
Maintaining Faith and Endurance in Challenging Times

Notes:

_____

_____

_____

_____

_____

_____

_____

_____

PERSEVERRANCE UNDER PRESSURE
Maintaining Faith and Endurance in Challenging Times

_____

_____

_____

_____

_____

_____

_____

_____

_____

_____

Bibliography

Lockman Foundation. *Comparative Study Bible.* Zondervan Publishing House. Grand Rapids, MI, c1984

The Bible Library. *The Bible Library CD Rom Disc.* Ellis Enterprises Incorporated, (c) 1988 – 2000. 4205 McAuley Blvd., Suite 385, Oklahoma City, OK 73120. All Rights Reserved.

Merriam-Webster Online Dictionary. Copyright © 2005 by Merriam-

Webster, Incorporated. All rights reserved.

PERSEVERRANCE UNDER PRESSURE
Maintaining Faith and Endurance in Challenging Times

Notes:

PERSEVERRANCE UNDER PRESSURE

Maintaining Faith and Endurance in Challenging Times

_____

_____

_____

_____

_____

_____

_____

_____

_____

www.ingramcontent.com/pod-product-compliance
Lightning Source LLC
Chambersburg PA
CBHW050343010526
44119CB00049B/681